GUARDIAN
A true story based on the
Memoirs of
Antonio DiTommaso, Sr.

By Suzanne DiTommaso

ISBN13:978-0692479100
ISBN-10:0692479104

Outspan Publishing

CHAPTER ONE

May 2014 - Hubbard Ohio

It was a warm spring afternoon and Tony DiTommaso finished pulling some weeds from among his endive. The sun was getting warm as the afternoon drew on so he stood in the shaded area of his garden in Hubbard, Ohio. He wandered back and forth between the rows and investigated the height of his garlic. He wiped the sweat from his brow and sighed as he recognized the ache in his back as he straightened up. His stomach rumbled and he decided it was time for an afternoon break and something to eat. Brushing the dirt from his hands onto his faded blue jeans he made his way up the lawn. He heard her calling as he entered through the screened in back porch door which slammed behind him.

"Tone!" his wife, Patty called out from the kitchen window.

"Huh?" he shouted back.

"Phone."

Tony, an Italian immigrant, now in his early 70's slipped out of his dirty shoes and ambled across the carpet in his socks taking the cordless phone from Patty. "Thanks," he whispered and walked back out onto the back porch.

"Hello?" he said.

"Tony, this is Jack, Jack Frank. Umm I don't know how to start, well, you're never gonna believe this." The voice on the phone paused.

"Believe what?" Tony chuckled.

"There's a woman, in Lowellville. She's 80 years old. Tony." he paused again. "She thinks she knows you and she thinks you know her."

Tony's eyes scanned back and forth slowly over his garden in the distance as he tried to make sense of Jack's words. The next few sentences caused Tony to sit gently and silently in a chair at the back porch table. He stared at the floor, his head spinning. His face became flushed as he listened and he reached up and cupped his forehead with his free hand. His head dropped further as if weighed down by the conversation. Patty appeared in the doorway wiping tomato sauce from her hands with a dish towel. She became concerned by the look on his face.

"What is it Tone?" she whispered.

He could only stare at her and shake his head but she detected a slight smile.

"I often think back about my own young life. I was born in Italy in 1943 in the middle of the Second World War. It was just a small village called Baia e Latina . Baia e Latina is actually two small villages with a cemetery as common ground between them."

August 1943 - Baia e Latina, Italy

It was a hot August afternoon in the village of Baia e Latina in the Caserta region of Italy. In a tiny room on the second floor Gemma DiTommaso floated in and out of consciousness as the baby pushed against her womb. The sweat dripped down her face as the sound of American bombers thundered as they flew overhead. The bombers concerned the soon-to-be young mother as she cried out with every contraction. Her village had been heavily bombed during the war and most of the town is in ruins.

There was no electricity and no running water. Gemma DiTommaso was only 22 and really didn't know what future, if any there would be for her brand new son in the midst of this devastating war. She didn't know if there was a future for any of them if she was honest with herself but she could not worry about that. She cried out as the midwife encouraged her to push. She heard the tiny cries of her newborn son and collapsed back onto the hard stone floor.

The midwife used a damp cloth to clean the new baby. Gemma called out for her husband, Giovanni. Giovanni appeared in the door. His hands trembled as he moved toward his tiny new son. He'd never seen anything so fragile. He smiled at Gemma and wiped her forehead. "Antonio" he said and gently kissed his new son.

In the past several years Gemma and Giovanni's village had been invaded by German soldiers. Outside their little row house the sounds of bombs and explosions were ever present.

The American planes constantly bombarded the village, intent to kill as many Germans as possible. They killed much more than Germans however. The town's population was between 2100 and 2500 depending on the war conditions.

Baia was always littered with dead bodies and the buildings were destroyed one by one. The stench was ever present, especially in August.

Gemma, a short, stout young woman and Giovanni DiTommaso had married the previous year in 1942 during a double wedding. Young Gemma was married along with her sister Stephanie Ginocchi. Stephanie was similarly shaped with the same big, brown eyes. Stephanie married Simone a boy from the village. Gemma had two sisters, Stephanie and Annie who was not yet married. The ceremony was hushed and humble as German soldiers were camped on a nearby hillside and their threat was constant.

Many bombs and air raids plagued the village. The villagers had dug small bunkers into the hillsides and on many occasions Gemma and Giovanni along with other family members would be forced to run for the bunkers. Gemma would try to carry Antonio as long as she could and pass him onto Giovanni. Giovanni was so weak that often would have to pass the baby to his brother Modesto. This was the very reason Gemma's parents did not want her to marry Giovanni. His illness was undetermined but she was told he had a weak heart.

As her parents had feared, the marriage was short and ended tragically but not entirely unexpectedly when Giovanni DiTommaso died shortly after, when Antonio was only 14 or 15 months old. When her husband died Gemma was left a widow at 23 with a 14 month old baby and little to nothing else.

After Giovanni died, it was the baby's Uncle Pepino, Gemma's brother who was acting head of the house. He was also the one who showed the most interest in their safety because he knew how alone his sister was.

Gemma had another brother named Antonio. However, he died of a heart attack in Germany. Pepino was a scary man with a reputation for being quite violent.

As Antonio grew older he heard stories that he and his mother were taken prisoner by German soldiers and his mother was forced to cook for them and God knows what else. The story was that Uncle Pepino and his friends had some connections and knew where they were being held captive. One night they arrived with wine and sausage for the soldiers. Once the soldiers were good and drunk Uncle Pepino slit their throats and rescued Gemma and Antonio. Whether or not that was true, Antonio had no memory of that.

CHAPTER TWO

1947 Baia e Latina, Italy

"Some of my earliest and fondest memories were of my Grandfather and the way he would dance around the grape tub to make wine. Drinking wine, cupful after cupful he would wipe his big mustache. Another memory I have is me and him going to church on Sunday morning. The church was divided in three sections. The section on the right had all the statues of the different Saints and after service you would walk by, kiss your hand and touch them..."

It was early morning and Antonio's Grandfather Dominic Ginnochi was making his usual preparations for the yearly stomping of the grapes. Antonio, was watching an insect crawl slowly through the dirt and up a stone wall. The young boy, who was only 4 sat on a small wooden stool and watched the insect moving slowly up and up a long blade of grass. He sat in front of his grandparents' small two story farm house which was situated on 2 acres of land which they farmed.

They were very fortunate to have a house to live in as most of the village was destroyed by this point. The farmhouse sustained his grandparents, he and his mother, his great grandmother, and his aunts and uncles. It was very crowded.

Antonio's attention suddenly turned as his grandmother Rachel crested the hill with a bucket of water. Dominic Ginnochi was securing a giant wooden barrel on the dirt when he saw her arrive. Dominic turned to her and lifted one leg pointing his foot toward her. His pant legs were both rolled up and Grandma Rachel began to wash and scrub her husband's feet and legs. Antonio's mother Gemma and her sister Stephanie were standing nearby next to crates and crates of grapes they had picked from the vineyards on the farm.

"There!" Rachel said proudly. Grandfather Dominic stood up and lifted his leg over the side of the giant wooden barrel. He steadied himself and Rachel handed him a jug of the last year's wine and he took and very long chug.

He motioned to Gemma and Stephanie and they began to dump box after box of grapes into the giant barrel. As his grandfather stomped and stomped he sang and danced and Antonio smiled as he watched. His grandfather was a big man for those times and that part of the world. Antonio loved his grandfather, although, Dominic Ginnochi was not a reliable, stable sort of grandfather like most. He would disappear for weeks at a time and no one knew where he was but for that day he was there and he let everyone know it.

"My mother had two sisters. Aunt Stephanie was Gemma's younger sister and she had mastered the art of survival very well. During the war she was running across an open field to get away from the German soldiers. As she's running the soldiers were using her as target practice and one of the hit her right behind her ear and left her for dead. Somehow when she came to she found the rest of her family and they nursed her back to health. That bullet is still imbedded in her skull to today..."

"Bring the boy!" Antonio heard his grandfather shout. He had been stomping for some time and was quite drunk at this point and was pointing right at Antonio.

His grandmother Rachel shuffled over and knelt down before the little boy on the stool. Without looking at him she removed his only pair of shoes. His shoes were several sizes too big and he had them stuffed with paper to keep them from falling off. She slipped his shoes off easily and began to scrub Antonio's feet and legs.

Rachel lifted her grandson into the giant vat with his drunken grandfather. He looked up as the sun shone behind the head of Dominic blocking out most of his features. He could just make out a jug of wine being shoved at him.

"Drink!" Dominic shouted and let out a big bellowing laugh.

Antonio knew better than to disobey so he took a big chug of wine.

"Now stomp!' shouted his grandfather as he danced and stomped.

Antonio began to stomp around dizzily as he tried to avoid being trampled by his grandfather but occasionally felt the clumsy stomp of his grandfather's foot on his. For the rest of the morning he and his grandfather drank wine and stomped the grapes that would soon be the family wine.

When he was finally lifted out of the barrel Antonio made his way back to his little straw bed and slept for the rest of the day.

Fall 1947 - The kitchen of the Ginocchi Farmhouse- Baia, Italy

"The scene was like this. In my Grandparent's Ginocchi's little farmhouse was my Grandma Rachel, my Mother Gemma , me and my Uncle Peppino. My Uncle Peppino took his belt off and started beating my mother mercilessly. My Grandmother sat through the beating as if it was a common thing. My mother was screaming from the pain. My Uncle was screaming and swinging his belt like a wild man.... "

~

Antonio sat on a small stool in the humble kitchen of the family farmhouse. His little soon to be 5 year old legs could not reach nor were they welcome a the big table. His mother, Gemma was sitting at the small kitchen table and she was crying. His Uncle Pepino was shouting and was becoming more and more angry with every moment. The shouting made Antonio want to run from the house. He didn't dare move when his Uncle Pepino began to remove his belt. His eyes wide he watched his Uncle move toward his mother belt in hand.

The boy turned away as Gemma's brother began to beat her mercilessly. She screamed in agony and Antonio clapped his hands over his ears. He had no idea what she could have possibly done to make his Uncle so angry but he was too scared to move. He sat, eyes squeezed shut and tried to drown out the sounds of his mother crying. The beating went on for what felt like an eternity and finally his Uncle, physically exhausted from beating his sister left out the backdoor and the screen slammed behind him. His mother was slumped over the table and he could barely hear her crying. He dared not move as he sat, completely terrified, knowing his mother was hurting in ways he could never comprehend.

Several days later Antonio was told he must move in with his Uncle Pepino and his family. His mother was gone. Just gone. Where had she gone? What had happened to Gemma? He waited in the small dark kitchen until his Uncle arrived at the back door. He knew better than to ask any questions and silently left the farmhouse with the clothes on his back and nothing else.

He was brought into the family home and directed to his cousin's room. At his Uncle's house he had no bed so he was forced to sleep with his cousin Rachel in her crib. They slept head to toe and Antonio dared not make any complaints for fear his Uncle's belt.

Antonio started kindergarten that fall when he turned 5. He didn't know how long his mother had been gone but he knew it must have been a long time because he was older and the seasons were starting to change. He wanted to ask where she was but instead he became very efficient at listening and not being noticed. He was a silent member of the house and by being such he heard and learned everything.

Piecing information together he would retreat by himself and analyze the parts of conversations he was able to glean. His mother was in Naples? Why Naples? Over the next several weeks and months he discovered that his mother had been sent away to a home for unwed mothers. She was to have the baby, give it up for adoption and come back after she had nursed it. A boy. A brother. Antonio had no idea what to do with that information so he stored it in the deepest parts of his mind not knowing when or if he would ever want to access it again.

"I don't remember exactly when Gemma came back to Baia but we ended up in a two room house on the second floor of a building with a big courtyard. We had one room with a fireplace that was used for cooking and heating. There was a brick oven to bake bread in..."

CHAPTER THREE

1948 Baia e Latina, Italy

"One of my first memories of Baia is the majority of the people being infected with lice. Now in today's standards being infected with lice is bad enough but back then it was really bad. You see our little village was heavily bombed and the majority of it was destroyed..."

Antonio sat up in his bed and felt the sun hit his face through the window. He ran his fingers through his itchy, dark, curly hair and rubbed his eyes. His mother had returned from Naples without a baby and they had moved into a two room house on the second floor of a big courtyard. He was curious about what had happened to the baby but he was too young to really comprehend what had happened. He was however, feeling quite mature at six years of age and Antonio knew his morning would be spent mostly on his own. He shifted around and heard the scratching of the corn husks.

Gemma had sewn two sheets together and stuffed them with corn husks which was laid on the dirt floor and it was something Antonio was grateful for; a place to sleep. It was uncomfortable to say they least but the bigger problem was that it bred lice and lots of them.

Antonio continued to scratch his infested head and underarms and got out of bed. He wandered outside and headed to his "bathroom" area. He tottered down a steep set of stone stairs into the courtyard and down the past the heavily bombed buildings of Baia.

Outside the bombed out buildings were strings of laundry drying in the sun. He made his way down under the bridge where many of the other townspeople were relieving themselves. The stench was thick but he was used to it. When the village would have a great rain all the stench would get washed away and this was completely normal to the young boy. His one and only pair of shorts came equipped with a slit in the back so that he could relieve himself. He did his business and wandered back to their humble lodging quarters. There, he was looking for the water container to take to the well when he heard a man's voice.

"Clothes," said the man through the opening of the doorway.

Antonio knew what he meant and went outside into the street. A man was standing in the street with a large sprayer. The compliant boy removed all of his clothing and placed them in a pile with the many others. The man sprayed the clothes with some sort of chemical in the hopes of killing the lice.

He turned to Antonio. "Arms!" he commanded.

Antonio raised his arms and felt the cool mist of whatever kind of chemical was in that sprayer. Baths came twice a year to Antonio. One in the spring and one fall during which time he was taken to the river with a bar of soap. He figured it must not be time for a bath and he knew that the whole village was infested with lice. He had no reason to fear the chemical and he hated the feeling of those itchy lice so he was happy to oblige.

"*One time I was coming home from my Grandparents house and on the way I found a dead chicken on the road. I picked the chicken up and took it home.*

Gemma asked me where I got the chicken. I told her I found it on the road. She said "Are you sure you didn't steal it?" I assured her that I didn't steal it and she cleaned it and cooked it. That was like a feast..."

~

Gemma took many jobs to keep her and her son alive. Gemma had not been successful in her schooling. At that time, children went to school until the 5th grade and then went off to work by the time they were 12. Gemma was not only still in school when she was 14 but she had not been able to pass the first grade. On the first day of school when she showed up as a fourteen year old first grader her teacher told her to go home and go to work. She had no other options so of to work she went.

By late summer 1948 Gemma had had multiple jobs and had recently taken a job cutting wheat. Antonio would follow along behind her. The wheat had to be cut very quickly so that the kernels did not fall to be stolen by birds so the workers moved very quickly with their sharp sickles flying back and forth.

One afternoon while following along in the wheat field Antonio heard his mother cry out and saw blood gushing from her finger. A couple of the other workers noticed and came to help. Someone tore a piece from her skirt and tied it around as a tourniquet. Just then a voice from the back shouted.

"Have Antonio pee on it!" Antonio looked at his mother, eyes wide. She paused and looked at him and suddenly began to nod her head. Antonio's eyes got very wide as he realized she was serious. So, as he had no choice, Antonio peed on his mother's finger right there in the open field. Another memory was pushed back into his mind, possibly forever.

The young mother and son lived on very meager rations. Mainly they ate polenta and bread. Once the wheat and corn had been completely harvested for the day Gemma was given permission by the field owner to scrounge for kernels. These kernels were taken to the grain mill and after the miller had taken his due Gemma was given what was left. As she had very little wood to burn in order to bake she would stockpile the cornmeal and flour until she had enough to make a large quantity. The bread was reasonably good when it was fresh but after a few days, or a few weeks it was very hard.

One of Antonio's jobs was to retrieve one of the loaves and wrap it in Gemma's handkerchief. He was to bring it with them and then find a stream somewhere near where his mother was working. He would place the bread in the stream and weight it with a rock so that throughout the day the bread would become saturated with water and therefore able to be eaten. His mother would open the bread and slice a few onions and they would eat right there in the field.

Young Antonio had several jobs while he followed his mother in the fields. One of them was to catch birds for dinner. Someone had provided him with a spring loaded trap which he became very skilled at using. He would place a piece of bread in the trap and soon he would hear a "snap".

Often he would catch a sparrow or a robin and over the course of the day he might catch 4 or 5 small birds. On those evenings his mother would pluck and gut the birds, cut off their little beaks and feet and boil them. This was considered a good day.

"One year we got a baby pig about six weeks old. During that summer my job was to tie a rope on the pig's front foot, put the pig in a ditch along the road and let it eat the grass. I would hold the other end of the rope so the pig didn't run away. BORING, BORING, BORING..."

~

Antonio grumbled under his breath as he held the end of the skinny rope tied to the pig. The sun was so hot that day and he was so thirsty. He had no hat or shade so he wandered back and forth kicking the long grass and just hoping for the day to pass quickly. He felt like he had done nothing but stand it that ditch for days. He was right.

"Stupid pig..." he mumbled, resenting the pig. "We're going to eat you, you know."

Just then, he heard a rustling behind him. He squinted as he turned and looked across the ditch. Another small pig! He wondered where that pig had come from and his eyes scanned up. Much to his surprise and delight he looked directly into the eyes of a young girl. Apparently, she had been given the same exact job. To hold the pig rope. The two became fast friends and made plans each day of where to meet. They would chat and keep each other company while the pigs fattened. They grew closer all summer long. His first crush, his first love. She was affectionately referred to throughout his entire life as "pig girl."

CHAPTER FOUR

"One day a horse drawn cart came to town. In the cart was a driver and a female passenger who had come from America and she came to visit her family. Her name was Mary Mastrioni. She was born in Baia and then immigrated to Hubbard, Ohio. She had come to spend a month to see her family but she really took a liking to Gemma..."

Antonio watched his mother and Mary walk toward the horse drawn cart. The two had spent so much time together in the month that Mary had been there. Antonio was sitting on a small stone wall, kicking his legs harder and harder as he watched. Mary didn't seem to be worried about saying goodbye to him and he didn't much care.

The two women embraced. He knew Mary was leaving and going back to America. He wondered what America must be like. He had heard stories but couldn't imagine that world.

"I'm going to find you a husband in America." Mary said brushing Gemma's hair back off her dusty face." Gemma smiled shyly and did a grateful half bow. Mary got on the cart and the horse lunged forward.

"I will write. I will," she said convincingly as the horse pranced around anxious to go. Mary smiled at Gemma and waved. Antonio watched the cart start up slowly, gain speed and eventually disappear around the corner. He doubted he would ever see her again.

Several months passed. One day as Antonio was sitting on the stoop, the mail cart arrived. The man on the cart said there was a letter for Gemma. Antonio ran up to the man and took the letter.

"Mama!" He called for her as he entered the small house. Gemma was by the fire making some sort of mushy bread out of polenta. Gemma stood up and snatched the letter from her young son's hand. Her eyes scanned the front of the envelope and she stared at the postage stamp. She looked around the room excitedly and then she ran to find her sister, Stephanie. Gemma could not read and Stephanie was her only hope to find out if Mary Mastrioni had kept her promise.

The letter was from a man in America. A man named Jim.

"*Jim and Mary were friends and neighbors so they knew each other very well. Jim lived with his daughter Mini, his son in law Charley and three grandchildren, Chuck, Dee and Jimmy. The odd thing was Jim was sixty three years old and Gemma was twenty nine. That's a big difference.*"

~

Shortly after the first letter arrived Antonio and Gemma made the horse and cart journey to Caserta. There was a photographer there and he was told they would need a photograph of the both of them to send to Jim. Antonio went along with it, just as he had always done. He had very little control or say over what went on in his life.

Over the course of several months Gemma and Jim wrote back and forth. Jim Condi was much older than Gemma. He was divorced and lived in a town called Hubbard which was in a place called Ohio. All the while Stephanie was in the middle because she did all the reading, translating and writing. She made sure all the mail came directly to her so she could translate.

Jim had apparently proposed to Gemma at some point because Antonio learned that he was coming to Italy and that there would be a wedding. Stephanie was making all the arrangements and controlling everything as she had always done.

July 1952 Baia - Italy

It was early one morning after a big rainstorm had come through Baia. Antonio had been sent with his bucket to the hillside to collect snails. After a strong rain the snails would either fall off the rocks or they would be easier to pry off. He poked and pried with his little knife at a small, wet snail just as it popped off the rock and landed hard with the others. He looked down into his wooden bucket. He had quite a collection and he wondered if it was enough for his mother to cook for dinner that night.

He stood up and wiped his brow. He decided he was tired of collecting snails and it would have to be enough. He turned and carefully made his way down the slippery rocks in his bare feet and headed back to the village. Just as he turned the corner and started down the little street back to his house he saw a horse drawn cart arriving on the other end. Antonio heard a commotion in the street and ran to see what was happening. As he neared he could see a parade forming. A man was standing on the back of the cart yelling "Fish for sale!'" Antonio never understood why he had been saying that but people started to follow the parade to Stephanie's house. He followed behind as fast as he could without swinging his bucket of dinner snails. The man was Jim and he had come from America to marry Antonio's mother.

Jim stayed in Stephanie's house with her family while the wedding arrangements were made. In the house were her husband, Simone, her father in law, and two sons, Raphael and Dominico. Stephanie had not done a very good job in sorting out the details because when Jim and Gemma went to speak to the priest they were told that they could not be married because Jim was divorced and Gemma's husband had not been dead for ten years. Aunt Stephanie scrambled and made some sort of deal with a local government official to come to the house and perform the wedding.

The day of the wedding Antonio stayed in the shadows of the very crowded house. Most weddings he had seen were held outdoors but this time all the adults were staying indoors. Jim and Gemma were married in the very small front room with dirt floors. Stephanie had prepared a huge meal and the table looked very delicious to the young, hungry boy.

Aunt Stephanie called all the wedding guests to the dinner table after the ceremony but just as they all sat down to eat they heard a noise begin to grow outside. The adults all became very anxious and Antonio watched as they all loudly discussed what to do. Antonio could hear men shouting and he ran to the window. There was a large crowd in the street below the window. They all had pots and spoons and anything that would make noise and the crowd grew bigger and bigger as they protested the wedding of Jim and Gemma. That was their custom when anyone who had been divorced got remarried.

"I can remember a man riding a mule up and down the street, drinking and beating on some sort of metal pot. The mule got scared as he did this and went faster and faster. Finally the adults in my Aunt's house got buckets of wood ashes and dumped them on the men. Some of the ashes had hot coals which burned the men. Finally they locked the doors and windows and tried to go to sleep, but you could hear the commotion outside way into the morning."

Several days after the wedding as things were just starting to calm down and get back to normal, a horse and cart arrived outside the house. Antonio watched as Jim gathered his very few belongings and he and Gemma walked out to the cart. They said goodbye and he was gone. He'd gone back to America.

"I assume he and Gemma talked about their plans. I didn't know anything about them. All I thought I knew was 'One day I'm going to America.'

Things for Gemma got very difficult after Jim left. Antonio would watch as Gemma worked harder and harder. It became obvious over the next few months that she was pregnant.

The sun was beginning to set and Antonio watched his heavily pregnant mother mix mortar in a bucket. She placed the full bucket on her head and once she was sure it was balanced she ascended the ladder to the second floor. Aunt Stephanie's father in law was in laying some block on the second floor of the building and had offered Gemma a little bit of money if she would help. She had been at it all day. She did this every day for weeks and weeks.

Other days he followed his mother to fields in the village and she would spade the fields. Other days she would gather laundry and do washing for whatever anyone would pay her.

"As I look back and think, I can't help but think that Jim would send money to Gemma and Stephanie would get the mail and pocket the money. Gemma had no way of knowing otherwise. "

CHAPTER FIVE

March 1953 Baia, Italy

Antonio stood outside the row house and watched his mother and his Aunt Stephanie. The time had come for her to leave. Gemma walked slowly and awkwardly to the edge of town and bent down. She hiked up her dress. She was barely able to squat as she was so pregnant by this time but she was determined. She stopped, looked around and leaned over. She made a big black cross in the road. This was to signify that she would never come back. She walked back to the cart and was loaded into a horse drawn cart with whatever little belongings she had. Antonio was told she was going to America. His mother and his Aunt Stephanie set off for Naples where Gemma would board a ship called Queen Elizabeth.

"For me Gemma's leaving was no big thing. In today's world if you could imagine an 8 year old being left behind by his mother you would probably imagine a party, hugs, kisses, crying, not the case. For starters, this was not the first time I was left behind...

After Gemma left things got much harder for Antonio. He moved in with his Aunt Stephanie and felt like an outcast. Grandmother Rachel died that summer and that led to arguments about the division of the land. Not long after Antonio moved in he was told he was no longer going to school. Antonio would be sent to work with the men and Stephanie's son Raphael would go to school and make something of himself.

He spent most of his time alone dreaming of America. The young boy had the distinct feeling that his Aunt was not happy about taking care of him and she only did it for financial gain. His grandfather was being passed around the family with nowhere to live after Rachel died. The family came up with a rotating schedule wherein he would stay for three months. The family members would feed him and provide him all the wine he wanted and he would move on to the next hosts. Antonio was sure his mother must have been sending him money but he never saw any of it.

One evening Antonio overheard his Aunt discussing his future in America. He tried not to be noticed as he listened behind the door. Stephanie was loudly describing a letter she was writing to Gemma and it said that if Gemma didn't send a certain sum of money Stephanie would not do the paperwork on her end for Antonio to come to America.

"Now that was a scary thought. Going to America was a dream. It was the promised land. My Grandfather would tell stories about the abundance of everything in America, especially food. By the time he got done telling his story he had your mouth watering. I wanted to go to America. Every day got a little bit harder for me..."

Antonio was struggling to find his place in the family and in the world in general. If he was not going to America, if his mother was not coming back, what would happen to him? He was accustomed to poverty, hunger and lack but he knew that if his mother did not send for him he had very little hope. He began to act out and became defiant. He would argue and shout at his Aunt and Uncle. He hoped every day for the news that he was leaving for America but each day he was disappointed. Spring turned to summer and summer turned to autumn. The young boy was sent out daily into the fields to work and was told not to come back until the sun was setting.

Winter set in and there was less to do in the fields. Antonio would sit in his Aunt Stephanie's house by the fire day in and day out hoping for spring, hoping for news, hoping for anything. When spring finally did arrive the family resumed their normal routine and went out to plant the fields.

It was late spring as Antonio was standing in a giant field of tomato plants. He bent down and looked for any signs of new tomatoes but saw nothing but flowers. He was actually relieved by this because his mother had always smacked him for picking tomatoes. He was supposed to pick tomatoes but she yelled at him when he did. He did not understand and was always very nervous when he was sent to tend to the tomatoes.

"Why are you picking green tomatoes?" she would shout while smacking him in the back of the head. "Look! Look!" she would point the fruit on the vine.

The confused child would look at the tomatoes. They all looked the same to him. It was not until many years later that he learned that he was color blind. That certainly explained a lot of things.

Antonio spotted his Aunt Stephanie approaching from a distance. He knew he had better look busy so he bent down and started pulling on a very stubborn weed at the base of a very tall tomato plant. He looked out the corner of his eye as he saw her marching toward him, apron swinging with great purpose and intention. He heard her breathing hard as she arrived in the middle of the field of tomatoes. He kept his head down wondering what he had done this time but he was not looking forward to whatever had caused her to tramp out through the field to confront him. He stood up slowly and looked at her.

"It's time. Your mother has sent for you. You are going to America." She said breathlessly and leaned down holding her knees. Antonio felt his heart leap in his chest. Finally.

News of Antonio's trip to America spread quickly through the village of Baia. Most of the villagers were genuinely excited for him. The local barber offered him a free haircut and the local shoemaker made him a pair of shoes for the journey. Antonio was told he was being taken to Caserta to have a passport photo taken but he had nothing to wear.

"There was an American family that came to Baia to visit family. That family had a young boy about my age and size and that boy had a sweatshirt, with Hopalong Cassidy on the front. I thought that would be a nice picture with Hopalong Cassidy riding his horse and throwing a lasso over his head. So I stole it and had my passport photo taken in it."

Antonio didn't see much of his Grandmother DiTommaso, presumably because his Dad had died when he was just a baby. But, he had been sent to Cungetta DiTommaso's house to say goodbye before he left for America.

Grandma DiTommaso was holding Antonio by each shoulder as she smiled and took in every feature of his face.

"What will you wear to America?" She said excitedly with tears in her eyes. Antonio shrugged. Grandma took a big deep breath and smiled.

"I still have your father's wedding suit," she let go of Antonio and plodded across the room to a small chest. She pulled out an old suit. It was creased and looked like it had been folded for a very long time.

"It's too big," Antonio said staring at the suit.

"I can make it fit," she said enveloping Antonio in the jacket and forcing his arm down each sleeve. She lifted each foot and placed it in each pant leg and pulled the pants up over Antonio's small frame. She hiked up the pants as far as she could and cinched his waist with the belt's loose end hanging down his leg. She pulled each arm forward and rolled up each sleeve.

"Stand up straight," she said and Antonio complied. He felt her cutting the bottom of the pants. She cut the pants off at the ankles with scissors and the crotch was at his knees. She stood back and smiled at him. He must have looked quite a sight but she smiled seeing her own son as she imagined what Antonio would look like one day.

Antonio kissed his Grandmother DiTommaso and said goodbye. She squeezed him tight as she tearfully said goodbye. Antonio didn't really have any expectation of the future but his Grandmother knew she would never see him again.

Antonio went back to Aunt Stephanie's house and dreamed about America that night. There was so much food. There was so much everything! He could hardly sleep out of sheer excitement.

It was before dawn the next morning and the anxious boy couldn't sleep. He scrambled out of bed and put on his father's wedding suit. It was huge but it was all he had to wear. He went outside in the dark street and looked around the town. He had no way of knowing what time it was or what time he was going to America so he sat outside and watched sun come up. His Aunt appeared in the doorway and he looked up at her.

"They are coming to get us. Are you ready to go" she looked down at the boy.

Antonio looked down at his empty hands "I'm ready," he said.

The boy in the ill fitting suit and Stephanie walked toward the horse and buggy. Antonio looked down the street to the place where his pregnant mother had made the big black cross in the road. He smiled to himself, turned and climbed straight up into the cart.

CHAPTER SIX

June 1954 - Eastern coast of Italy.

Antonio sat quietly next to Stephanie and stared out at the Italian coastline as the train rattled along the track. He watched the sun dancing off the ripples in the water of the Tyrrhenian Sea. The Italian countryside was all he had ever known and he had never seen the sea but he was so ready to leave. They had already traveled by horse and buggy to get there but he had no idea what other types of transportation he would be using. He knew about the ship but then what? He tried not to think about it. He didn't know how long the journey to the promised land would be.

The train was crowded and hot. He looked around at all the faces. Most seemed to be families or couples with lots of trunks, luggage and bags. The strangers all traveled the long journey down the coastline from Baia e Latina to Naples where Antonio had been told he would get on a ship and travel alone to America. The nervous boy looked around the train at the many faces. He wondered if any of them would be with him on the ship. He looked for anyone his age and he imagined what the journey might be like.

The train clanked on and Antonio looked up at his Aunt as she stared straight ahead, rocking back and forth with the motion of the train. As if sensing him, she looked down at him and forced a smile. The smile did little to comfort him as he had no idea what his future held. He forced a smile and looked back out the window. He thought of his Dad who had died years earlier while Antonio was a baby and summoned up all the courage in his little 10 year old heart.

He daydreamed of America and his mother who had gone on before him. The people were packed in and Antonio felt very small. He tried to go to sleep but he was awakened with every stop. The journey dragged but eventually he could see they were getting close to Naples.

Soon, the train pulled up to the station in Naples and Antonio and his Aunt made their way through the roped off lines and out to the Naples shipyard. There were ruins of buildings all around from the bombings but on one side of the port were enormous ships. The sun shone brightly that day. It was very hot and the sky was clear and blue.

Antonio's eyes widened as he stared up at the giant ship, a ship bigger than anything he could have imagined. The crowd was noisy and it seemed chaotic. He heard all different languages and people were going in every direction. Aunt Stephanie turned to Antonio. She handed him his passport and papers. "Don't lose anything. You can't get to America if you lose these papers. Tell your mother to write to us when you get there," she said.

The port was massive, big ocean liners docked all along the street, people coming and going from different countries, you would hear different languages, you seen different clothes. Then you had the gypsies and the hustlers. You had to watch your pockets, a good street hustler could cut your wallet out without you feeling or knowing a thing until it was too late. This I know first hand.

Antonio looked down at his "papers". He folded them and shoved them deep into his front pocket because he knew about thieves and pick pockets. He didn't know what they said but he knew they were important.

As they made their way through to the front he noticed a long wooden gangplank and hundreds of people lining up. His Aunt Stephanie had remained quite stoic throughout the journey. "Addio". She said and motioned him toward the ship.

She hugged him and then nudged him again forward toward the gangplank. Everyone was so much taller than he was and he felt alone as he stumbled forward looking up at the other passengers. He tried to figure out how to get to the end of the line.

Antonio watched as big pallets of food were being loaded through a cargo door. He could just make out the letters on the giant ship's hull. Conte Biancamano. Shipyard workers bustled around as the passengers destined for America stood in the beating sun waiting to board. He looked up at the giant ship's smokestack which suddenly blew out black smoke. He took his place in line and smiling he turned back to wave at Auntie Stephanie. She was nowhere in sight.

May 2014 ~ Lowellville, Ohio

It was a warm spring morning. Before dawn Gerbina DiRienzo woke up abruptly from her sleep. She laid in bed listening to the light patter of spring rain on the roof as she stared at the ceiling. Gerbina, an Italian immigrant felt the familiar ache of unanswered questions of her past. For years she had thought of him and dreamed of the journey. The ache seemed to be greater as time went by. She would be 80 this year.

She felt the great divide of time. She felt the familiar twinge of heartache as she thought about her husband Joe. He'd been gone two years. How could that be? Time seemed to have created two different worlds and yet the big ship seemed like yesterday. Every detail was untarnished in her mind.

Gerbina got up and made her way into her Lowellville kitchen. She had been living in that house for nearly 60 years. She knew every inch of the kitchen. How many pots of sauce and cannolis she had made there.

She had raised her two children, Bina and Guy in that house with her beloved husband, Joe. Grandchildren and great grandchildren had been a result of the loving marital bond in that house in Lowellville, Ohio.

She had lived a long and wonderful life in America and yet, somehow she was unable to shake the longing to know what had happened to him.

CHAPTER SEVEN

June 1954 ~ Port of Naples, Italy

Antonio wiped the sweat that was dripping from his jet black hair. His undershirt was wet but he decided to keep his jacket on. He glanced down and shuffled his feet noticing the fraying of the hem of his father's suit pants. His Grandmother must have cut a lot of fabric from those suit pants to make them fit him. He glanced around at all the people with their bags and trunks. He had no bag, no trunk, just the clothes on his back and his "papers".

Someone was shouting out orders and instructions. The passengers were told they would board them alphabetically and Antonio was shoved into his place in line. He dared not speak to anyone. He slowly and silently shuffled his feet along as the line moved forward. It seemed hours later when he found himself at the front of the line to the man in uniform who was checking paperwork. Antonio was both excited and scared to embark on this journey across the ocean but he was certainly ready to get out of that line.

"Papers," said the man in the uniform abruptly.

Antonio reached out his armful of papers and the man looked at him suspiciously. The man's eyes scanned the nearby passengers.

"DiTommaso, where are your parents?" he said with authority.

"My Mother is in America and my Father is dead," Antonio said nervously.

"You can't get on this ship without a chaperone!" the man said astonished. "Unaccompanied minors cannot board this ship," he said as if he needed to clarify. He looked down at the boy. "You need an adult to sign for your well-being young man. I'm sorry son, you'll have to get out of the line."

Antonio was dumfounded. Now what? He looked back to the pier and couldn't see anyone he knew. His aunt was long gone. He turned to the man behind him. He looked down at the papers. Not really understanding what was required but knowing that he needed someone to sign he looked up at the man who didn't look very likely to help.

"Sign my papers sir?" the man pushed past Antonio as if he didn't hear him.

He turned to the next man in line.

"Sign my papers sir, please." the man shook his head and gestured for Antonio to get out of his way. Antonio was getting very scared and desperate. People started to shove him out of the line. He heard their jeers and the steward told him he was holding up the other passengers.

"Unaccompanied minors cannot board this ship," said the steward once again but this time he had a hold of the boy's thin arm. The steward gave Antonio's arm a giant shove and he stumbled out of line.

Just then a gentle hand touched his shoulder. He looked up into the beautiful face of young woman with dark hair all pulled back in a bun. She was modestly dressed and she had a warm smile. She bent down so she could see him face to face.

"What's wrong little boy?" she asked warmly.

"I can't get on the boat alone. But, I am alone, " Tony said with a lump forming in his throat and tears forming in his eyes.

Her heart was filled with compassion. Although she had no children of her own yet, she knew that she and her husband, Joe planned to have many children when they were reunited in America.

"What is it you need? Someone to sign your papers? I'll sign your papers boy," she whispered smiling.

She stood up suddenly "I'll sign his papers!" she shouted to the man in uniform grabbing Antonio by the hand and forcing her way to the front. Dragging Antonio behind her she shoved grown men out of the way as she stood boldly in the face of the man in uniform.

"How old are you?" said the steward suspiciously as she stood in front of him.

"I'm 20 years old. I'm a married woman, I can certainly be the guardian for this boy."

He paused and looked at her and then to the papers she had shoved out in front of her.

"Ok Miss, if that's your choice," he said patronizingly, " He's your problem now." The young woman quickly signed the papers. The man inspected their papers, stamped both of their passports and gestured for them to get on. Antonio followed very closely behind the young woman.

May 2014 -Lowellville, Ohio

Gerbina and her family sat down at a small table in a local restaurant as they prepared to hear Gerbina's great nephew's band play. Gerbina looked distraught and her niece recognized that familiar look on her face.

"What is it?" asked her niece, Darlene.

Gerbina shrugged.

"No really, what is it? You don't seem yourself today."

Gerbina looked into her niece's eyes.

"I dreamed of the boy again." She looked down into her lap sadly.

"Oh, that was 60 years ago, we keep telling you that you can't worry about him anymore, he would be a grown man."
.

"I just don't know what happened to him? Should I have stayed with him? Did his mother find him?" Gerbina continued.

Jack Frank and his wife Stephanie who were sitting with the family overheard Gerbina's distress. "What's wrong?" He asked seeing that the two women were distraught.

"There was a little boy on the ship when Gerbina came over from Italy in 1954. She's worried about him for years."

"A little boy?" Said Jack

"Yes, his name was Antonio. She left him on the dock at Ellis Island. We think he's in Brooklyn somewhere but sometimes she just feels guilty for leaving him there. Uncle Joe was waiting for her and naturally she was excited to see him. Married people had to go to a different line at immigration so she had to leave the little boy. I keep telling her she can't feel bad about that..."

"Wait. Did you say his name was Antonio or maybe Tony?" Jack stopped and stared at the women.

"Yes." they both said in unison.

"...and he was all alone?"

The women nodded.

CHAPTER EIGHT

June 1954 - Puerto de Napoles, Italia

The passengers were all filing onto the great ship. The young woman and Antonio made their way up the ramps and were happy to be in the shade at various times. There was a lot of hurry up and wait as the thousands of passengers boarded the great ship.

They came to a steward who asked to see their tickets. Antonio looked at his ticket which read "Biglietto d'imabarco di Terza Classe". The young woman produced her ticket and was waved onboard. Antonio handed his ticket to the steward. "No room in third class." He said and handed Antonio a slip of paper
"Third class if full." He said as if repeating himself.
Antonio could not read or speak English and he looked at the Steward and down at the paper.
"Biglietto d'imbarco di second class, Cabin 663," said the Steward.

The young boy looked up. "I can't get on?" He looked up at the kind young woman who had come to his aid. "Yes, you can get on, in fact you've just been upgraded you lucky boy," she said smiling. "Come on, follow me." She put a hand on his shoulder pulling him onto the ship.

The young woman led Antonio through the enormous ship and eventually arrived at Cabin 663. "Well, you certainly are a lucky boy," she said looking at his cabin door. "You've been upgraded from third class to second class. I heard the food is better, " she said winking. "You stay here," she said to him calmly. "You'll be ok here and I'll see you soon."

Antonio apprehensively entered the cabin where three men were unloading suitcases and trunks.

The young boy noticed a bed with nothing on it and sat on the bed. He looked nervously at the men. They were joking and laughing and didn't seem to pay much attention to his arrival.

Soon he heard the giant steamship's horns blowing and Antonio heard a great deal of excitement in the hallways. He ran out to the ship's railing to see if he could wave to his Aunt. He couldn't see her anywhere but he decided to stay right where he was. He felt very small and he could see nothing but a giant ocean ahead of him.

There were people everywhere, hanging on the balconies waving goodbye. People crying, some out of happiness, some out of fear of the future. This lasted all afternoon. Finally the big ship sounded its massive air horns a few times and then you felt movement. Four tugboats were pulling this massive ocean liner out to sea. Finally the tugboats turned the big ship loose and you felt the ship pick up speed. I stood in the same spot, looking for my aunt, never to see her again.

As it got dark I was still on the balcony looking all the time at the water, and it finally hit me. Where am I going? How am I getting there once I get off this big ship?

He was tired from the day. He stayed there until dark and made his way quietly back to his cabin. He was hungry but decided he would rather sleep than go back out with all those strangers and figure out how to find food. He tucked his papers under his pillow and looked down at this shoes. Nervous someone would take them, he slipped off his shoes and tucked them in with him under the sheet. He laid his head back on the pillow and peered out from under the sheet around the room. He continued to hear the other passengers milling around the hallways excitedly. He began to think again about what America would be like but it was only moments and he was sound asleep.

SS Conte Biancamano - 1954

"The next morning the ship anchored at a different port. Some people got on and some people got off. Later that day it left port again for a new destination. On our way to America the ship made numerous stops along the way.

I remember Sicily, France, Portugal, Spain, England and Canada. The trip itself took thirteen days and fourteen nights. It was a long trip, but the good part was there was lots of food.

Good food, food that I had never seen or heard of. The first few days I couldn't eat enough and being in the second class part of the ship, you got better food than you did in third class...which is where I was supposed to be anyhow."

Antonio spent most of his time walking up and down the ship's decks. Staying in the cabin was very boring and Antonio wandered up and down the decks most of the days.

Sometimes he would go down to the Third Class passengers and talk to kids his age. He had figured out the dining routine and was overjoyed by the amount of food he could eat. The Second Class food was better than anything he had ever had in his whole life. The food was good but had not figured out how to wash. He couldn't take his clothes off as he was still apprehensive to lose his father's suit or his shoes. Even if there were a laundry room what would he wear while he washed his clothes?

One very hot afternoon he was walking on the ship's deck and stopped to watch the people swimming in the big swimming pool. He was incredibly hot. The sun was reflecting off the pool water. He walked up to the pool's edge. He looked left and right and stepped up on the ledge. He closed his eyes, took a big breath and jumped in with all his clothes on. It was a wonderful cool sensation as he felt the cool water surround him. As he surfaced he could hear whistles. He came to the edge of the pool he could feel hands grabbing his arms and pulling him out.

The young woman heard the boy's name being called on the loudspeaker. She sat up concerned and her heart leapt when she also heard her name being summoned to the Ship's Captain.

She asked a deck hand where to go and he directed her to the front of the ship. Upon arrival she was told by the First Officer that the boy had jumped in the ship's pool with all his clothes on.

"It's hot," she said to the First Officer trying not to giggle.

"Yes, it's not permitted."

"Ok, I'll see to it." she said and put an arm around Antonio's shoulder and guided him out the door smiling back at the First Officer.

Once outside she leaned down. "Don't do that again or we'll both be in trouble." she whispered to him and winked.

"I won't," he said and smiled back at her.

"You come and get me if you need anything, ok?"

"Ok," he replied and smiled shyly at her.

The young woman watched him daily but didn't interact much with him. They would catch eyes and smile at one another. They were strangers and yet they were sharing this journey and this experience together on many levels. The young woman found joy in watching the boy. He seemed quite happy and she hoped that he would have a happy life in America. She was looking forward to reuniting with her husband Joe who had gone on before and sent for her. He had sent word that he had a job and he had a place for them to live. They had already planned to have children and the young woman was excited to start their new life in America. The rest of the trip the young woman continued to watch the boy and make sure no one gave him any trouble and that he didn't get into any mischief. Neither happened.

"The third class section was one big room with bunk beds around the sides, and lines of beds through the center. It was like a big commune. Men, women and children lived and slept in the same room. It was a very busy, noisy place but for me it was a comforting place.

We had no T.V.'s or radios so the days were spent talking about "America" and how it was going to be. Everybody had dreams. Some people, if not most sold everything they had to pay for this trip. Most of them just had the clothes on their backs. One thing we all had in common was we all had dreams of America."

One afternoon Antonio was wandering around the third class section of the ship. Suddenly he noticed a lot of people congregating in the center of the room and it looked like a giant party. He learned that no food was permitted to be taken on shore. Many passengers had brought prosciutto, sausage and cheeses for their relative and when they settled in their new homes. All sorts of meat and cheeses were just being handed out and it was a giant picnic.

Afterward many people scurried to clean up for arrival. Antonio made his way up onto the ship's deck to see if he could catch a glimpse of America. He waited and waited until dark and finally went back to his cabin. But, several days later it happened.

"Early one morning I heard all kinds of commotion outside. I put my shoes on and opened my cabin door. There were people everywhere and they were all going to the deck. I followed the crowd outside and there it was; The Statue of Liberty. Men were crying, woman were waving their hankies to it. Whole family were kneeling down, holding hands and praying. I had no idea what was going on. At first I thought they were praying to a Saint. I saw a lot of people making the sign of the cross, So I thought it was some sort of Saint. I don't know if I figured it out or if somebody told me, but I finally got the picture. It was "America"! I was going to be rich! I would never go hungry again! I would have more than the clothes on my back! It was the promised land. It was AMERICA!"

The tugboats pulled the ship into the harbor and Antonio stared at the giant statue of a woman. His eyes scanned the crowd. Many men and women were weeping. It towered above the ship and it caused a great deal of emotion. The tugboats pulled and pulled and it felt like they were moving the ship one inch at a time. It came to a stop and Antonio heard a couple blasts of the air horns and the engines shut down. The workers started getting everything ready for disembarking and it finally hit the young traveler. Where was he going now? He was told he would get on a big ship but that was all he was told. He came to the very serious realization that he had no idea where he was going now!

CHAPTER NINE

Lowellville, Ohio 2014

"His name was Antonio?" Jack repeated his question.

"Yes. Antonio," replied Gerbina

"Jack looked at Gerbina's niece, Darlene. "That sounds an awful lot like Tony D's story," she said apprehensively.

"What year did you come here Gerbina?" He asked

"1954, I arrived at Ellis Island on June 24, 1954."

"What is it Jack? What are you thinking?" Stephanie inquired.

"Tony DiTommaso. He lives right over in Hubbard. He came over by himself in 1954. I don't know the name of the ship but what if? Oh wow. In fact, I could call him right now."

"Hubbard right up the hill?" asked Darlene, "Seriously? Jack?"

Jack was already dialing his cell phone. "Tony, this is Jack, Jack, Frank. Umm I don't know how to start..."

New York Harbor - 1954

Antonio was pushed to the back of the line as the giant ship docked and the announcement was made to depart the ship. First class was first, naturally. It seemed forever as they waited and Second Class was called to depart. The young woman slipped in beside him as they departed the ship. There were signs and people directing the new immigrants to various roped off areas. The two walked side by side for some time until they came to a place where they were told they had to part. Married persons were being corralled into a different line. The young woman squatted down in front of him.

"I have to go that way," she looked at him. "Do you know where to go?"

"Not really," Antonio said not exactly sure.

She took a deep breath and held both his hands. "Follow the directions," she said and squeezed his hands. "I hope you find your mother soon. Ciao."

"Ciao," he said. He was genuinely quite confused about who she was and why she had looked after him but he had to focus on where he was to go next.

The two walked in opposite directions. Antonio looking for any indication of where he should go.

"Papers," he heard the familiar command of a uniformed person and he reached up and handed his papers to the man.

"This way," said the man.

As the new immigrants stepped onto American soil some of them bent down and kissed the ground. They were kissing each other and wiping others tears.

The young woman looked back several times and saw Antonio disappear into the long lines. She stood on her tip toes and searched the crowd trying to find him but soon was being asked for her papers and directed to a different line. She was excited to see her husband but her heart was sad as she realized she would never see that little boy again. She said a little prayer that he would find his mother in New York.

Ellis Island June 1954

"Now we had to line up to enter Ellis Island for our inspection. As we lined up I didn't realize we were on an island.

We all lined up outside of this massive building and started inching forward. As you got closer to the big doors the nervousness started to stir inside of you wondering "what's next"? When you got inside you look around and all you see are wall to wall people. We were directed to stand inside of these black pipe rails.

As you inched forward you would reach a point now and then when somebody in authority would ask you for your papers and passport. They would look at it, stamp it and you would inch forward."

Antonio had been in the line for what seemed like days. He had no food and no water but he knew not to get out of that line. He just stood and stood as the line very slowly ground on.

At various stations along the way his mouth was examined, people looked in his ears and he was given countless shots. He saw many people crying and kissing the ground. But sometimes a name would be called out and that person would be pulled from the line and sent to another area. He knew families were being broken up and he felt sad as he heard women and children crying "Don't take them!"

Even at such a young age his heart broke for those he knew would be sent back, knowing they had sold everything to get here and he knew their lives would be hard and their families torn apart. He couldn't imagine being sent back.

"Ellis Island was like the gateway to Heaven, but you had to go through hell to get there. A few years back I visited Ellis Island for the first time and after fifty six years when I walked through those halls I got goosebumps all over me. It took a lot for me to not break down and cry. We were with another couple and if it wasn't for them I probably would have. "

Eventually he reached the processing area where he produced his "papers" again. He was asked a series of questions he did not understand and a translator helped. He waited and waited and when they were finally done with their physicals he was put in another line to get on a ferry. A ferry! Another boat? He had no idea he was on an island. Once they got off the ferry it seemed that everyone had somewhere to go and someone they knew but him.

He must have looked lost because a woman came and asked him if he knew where he was going.

"My mother is in America."
Antonio looked up at the friendly face.

"Where in America?" She asked.

"I don't know." Antonio said starting to feel quite scared.

"Well," she said softly "do you have any papers?"

He pulled his papers out of his front pocket and handed them over. She read over the papers and the woman pinned something to his collar. He waited and waited before being placed in a taxi and taken to a train station where he waited to board a train. Tired, hungry and getting increasingly more scared that this was not going to be what he had expected at all, he got up on his tip toes at the train ticket window. The thirsty boy boarded the train with the hundreds of other people. Still not knowing where he was going he followed the direction of the people he met and trusted he was on the right path and eventually his mother would appear.

Hubbard, Ohio 2014

"It was the Conte Biancamano - June 1954". Tony said into the phone.

Patty searched his face wondering why he looked so flushed.

"Jack, if you're messing with me, I'll kill you." he said laughing. "Ok, ok then. Yes. Well, I guess so...I mean yes. It can't be, but sure. Ok, let me know."

He hung up the phone and stared at Patty.

"Well?" she said curiously.

"Jack knows a woman in Lowellville. Her name is Gerbina DeRienzo and she came over in June 1954. She said she took care of a little boy on the ship... his name was Antonio...and he was traveling alone. He's arranging a meeting."

Patty gasped and put her hands over her mouth.

A train somewhere outside New York City 1954

~

"I must have really stunk because nobody sat with me. After 13 days and 14 nights without even taking my socks off, I can't imagine how I smelled, but that was never my concern, or worry."

The tired and hungry young boy slouched in his seat and exhaustion overcame him. He woke up to a tap on his shoulder and he looked up into the face of a young black porter.

"Papers," he said.

Antonio lifted up his papers and the porter looked at them briefly. He smiled at Antonio, handed them back and moved to the next person.

He was just drifting off when he felt the train lurch forward. He heard the steam whistle and tried to keep his eyes open. He looked out the window at his first real look at America. His stomach rumbled and he felt the emptiness. He only felt that for a few minutes as the exhaustion overtook him and soon he was sound asleep.

"By the next morning, I'm getting pretty hungry. It's probably been close to thirty six hours since I had any food or drink"

Antonio was drifting in and out somewhere between asleep and dehydration. Suddenly he felt the tap on his shoulder. He gasped and woke up abruptly. The train was not moving. The porter nudged his arm and pointed at the open door. Antonio looked out at the platform. He did not know where he was but he didn't have anyone else to trust so he nodded to the porter and moved to the door, down the stairs and stepped out on the platform of the Erie Terminal in Youngstown, Ohio. His eyes scanned back and forth around the platform area. He knew no one and saw no one he recognized anywhere in sight. He had never been so scared in all his life. Feeling tired and hungry he walked back and forth. When the crowd cleared he spotted a bench, made his way over and sat down on it. He sat and sat. He waited and waited. His stomach began to ache with a deep ache of hunger and he looked around for a garbage can he could look in to possibly find food. He didn't see anything and felt so alone. He wondered if he was even in the right place. His head drooped and he was looking down at the pavement wondering if the big dream, the hope of a future in America was over.

CHAPTER TEN

June 24, 1954 Youngstown, Ohio
~

I don't know how long I sat there, it could have been 20 minutes it could have been 2 hours. By this time I was so nervous and scared about everything that it didn't matter. I thought if I have to spend the night on this bench I will. If I get hungry, I'll have to find food. Then I heard "Antonio. Antonio." I knew that voice, it was my mother. I don't know why but I can remember that scene like it was yesterday.

My mother was there, my stepfather, Jim and his son in law, Charlie McCallen. We stood here looking at each other for a few moments and she said "Are you coming?"

Antonio followed the group to the car and climbed in. There was no great celebration, just awkward silence. This new little family was coming together and growing at a rate of speed none of them could even begin to process. The language barriers, the age difference, the extendedness of the group and the fact that they were true strangers to one another ensured that the early days were cautious at best.

The brand new family pulled up to Antonio's new home in America. They ambled up the path and into the house. Antonio was introduced to a whole lot of new people. He tried to smile politely despite his aching hunger and thirst and wondered who they all were.

Jim introduced Antonio to his new family.
"This is your half-sister Rachel, my daughter Minnie and her husband Charlie, their daughter Delores, son Charlie and their other son Jim."

Antonio would have to learn who most of these new people were but he understood that his sister, Rachel had been delivered the day that his mother arrived in America by a midwife. She was a tiny girl and she seemed to have a lot of problems.

The young boy began to settle into his new home in Hubbard. Things were better than they had ever been when Antonio was suddenly, and inexplicably, sent to New Castle to live with his Aunt Matrona. He didn't mind and complied. Aunt Matrona was the woman who used to send packages to Italy. He was driven there in Jim's old truck to where she lived in a neighborhood largely populated with Italian immigrants. Antonio was just happy to be able to communicate with the kids around town. She taught him how to take a shower and one night she arranged a special surprise...

"One evening my Aunt arranged it with a few of her friends to take us to an entertainment park. I think it was Kennywood. I had never seen the likes of it. The people, the flashing lights, fireworks, and the different rides it was amazing."

Several months went by and one warm Sunday evening Antonio was sitting on the porch with Aunt Matrona when he recognized his stepfather's truck.

His mother and Jim had come back to collect him. Antonio was driven back to Hubbard where he began to finally settle in for real in his new home. No one ever told him why he went to New Castle that summer but he did as he always had and let it roll off.

Antonio lived with Gemma, Jim and the rest of the family at the corner of Chestnut Ridge and Old 62. Not long after his moving in Jim walked Antonio up to the D'Angelo house where there was a big group of kids congregating outside and making a ruckus.

"What's his name?" said the biggest kid who had a dirty face and a baseball hat which shadowed most of the dirt.

"Antonio," his stepfather hollered.

""Oh, Tony!" said the boy knowingly, "come on, you can be on my team."

"Tony" as he soon was known spent the next few weeks navigating the ins and out of how to play baseball and learning the American language from the neighborhood kids, not very nice language.

In September Tony was walked up to the Chestnut Ridge School. Stepfather Jim took him to Mr. Alpin who was the sixth grade teacher and school Principal.

"This is Tony Condi," said his stepfather to the Principal.

'A new life, a new name, this really was the American Dream', Tony thought to himself.

He knew very little English except for what the local kids had taught him so he had a long way to go and he knew it. Mr. Alpin took Tony to Mrs. Hollanbenk where he stayed in First grade for six weeks and then to Second grade for another six weeks. From there, he went onto Third Grade with Miss. McClellan but that year Miss. McClellan became Mrs. Ryser.

"It was Mrs. Ryser's first year of teaching so you can imagine how challenging this had to be for her. She would get class started on a lesson or project and then she would bring me to the back of the room and teach me the alphabet. She would teach me how to pronounce words, the names of different animals, and she would always tell me to go home and practice…and I did. She once gave me a comic book to take home and keep to practice reading with. I wore it out and went around the neighborhood asking for used comic books. We didn't have a T.V and in evening I would practice with the comic books sounding the words out.

Mrs. Ryser was a real blessing. Through the years I have often thought what a special person she was in my life. She laid the foundation for me to learn the English language and eventually the American way of life. "

The following year Tony was moved to Fourth Grade for six weeks and finally Fifth Grade by which time he was pretty much caught up with the kids his age.

CHAPTER ELEVEN

Hubbard, Ohio 1955

~

"My Stepfather was a quiet person, he hardly talked but he was a good hard working man. The neighbors and family either called him Uncle Jim or Grandpa. I called him neither. Jim had a daughter from a previous marriage, Minnie. Minnie was a peach of a person. She was the type of person that if she couldn't say something nice, she would not say anything. She was married to Charley McCallen. Between them they had three children, Chuck, Delores and Jimmy and they lived next door. Chuck was the oldest and I think everyone's favorite. Chuck learned a lot from his Grandpa and his Grandpa could build almost anything.

One day I was working in the garden and Chuck came over to our house and brought me a bike. He said that he went to the town dump, salvaged some parts and put together a bike for me. As you can see, he learned a lot from his Grandpa."

It was a cold November morning when Tony woke up and started getting dressed for school. He reached for his trousers on the floor and pulled them on. He padded out into the hallway in his socks when he stopped. He listed carefully. Nothing. The house was dead quiet. Tony walked back and forth in the hallway. Usually he could hear someone else in the house. He had the distinct feeling he was alone so he ventured down the stairs to the kitchen. No one. He was all alone again. Feeling a little bit anxious Tony went out the back door and trotted across the lawn to Minnie and Charley's house. 'Where could everyone be?' he thought. 'Have I been left behind again?' He burst through the kitchen door and Minnie jumped at the sudden entry. She looked at Tony's worried face. She smiled.

"Everyone's gone! I don't know what happened!" Tony exclaimed.

"Everything is fine," she put her arm around Tony's shoulders. "Come and have some breakfast." She guided Tony over to the kitchen table with Chuck, Dee and Jimmy who were already eating scrambled eggs.

"What's going on?" Tony said nervously.

"Your mother's gone to the hospital," said Minnie. "She's having a baby."

"A baby!" He looked at the his three breakfast companions who were oblivious to his shock.

"Yes, a baby. Everything is fine and you're going to be a big brother." Tony thought for a moment about the last time he had heard his mother was having a baby. No baby ever arrived. He looked down at his eggs and tried to make his eleven year old brain understand just what was going on. He dismissed his thoughts about the baby and focused on his eggs. He had a lot of other things to worry about besides a baby who may or may not ever appear.

Several days later his mother and stepfather returned from the hospital but this time she did bring a baby. In fact she brought two babies! His mother had given birth to twin girls. Delores and Gina. Once again his family grew at a rate he could not fathom. At that age and at that time in his life Tony had different priorities. He said hello to his brand new sisters and turned his focus to building his new American life.

"Today I stop to think about how my stepfather had to feel. In 1955 he was sixty eight years old, has a thirty four year old wife, a twelve year old stepson, who has been alone most of his life and doesn't listen very well. He has a four year old daughter who is mentally challenged and now twin girls. As I write this I am sixty eight years old so I can relate to his situation. All I can say is I don't know how he coped. No retirement benefits, a little bit of social security benefits, which wasn't much and now he's feeding a family of six. "

The family planted big gardens every year and they would go house to house in Sharon, Brookfield and Sharpsville to sell the produce. They would go to bars around the area around quitting time and intercept the workers before they spent all their money on beer. Their biggest seller was garlic. One year they had a thousand strings of garlic. Tony also had a paper route and he had to bring home the money he earned for his stepfather. In the summer and into fall they would cut wood and that would feed the furnace all winter to keep the family warm.

"My stepfather was a survivor. Life would knock him down and he would get back up and then life would knock him down again and he would get back up. The story about Uncle Jim or "Pa" as he was known goes like this..."

When Jim Condi was a young man, long before he had ever heard of Gemma Condi he was married once before. He married a woman who already had a daughter from a previous relationship and the daughter's name was Phyllis. Jim and his young wife ran a boarding house which was common in those days. Jim's young wife took a liking to one of the boarders and was having an affair known or unbeknownst to Jim, no one really knows. Jim's wife concocted a plan to get rid of Jim so she could be with her lover. She decided she would poison Jim, which she did and left him for dead. Apparently she had not given him enough poison and someone found Jim passed out, clinging to life and got him the medical attention he needed. He survived that attempt on his life and to everyone's shock and amazement he forgave her. They continued to run the boarding house and even had a daughter together. They named her Amelia or Minnie.

When Minnie was about 18 months and her half sister, Phyllis was a couple of years older their mother did it again! This time she poisoned Jim, took her daughter Phyllis, left Minnie behind and ran off with a man from Rome, Italy never to be seen again!

Jim was found unconscious by his sister who had come by the house to visit. Everyone called her "Grandma Marshall" and when she arrived Jim was left for dead on the kitchen floor. Little Minnie had apparently found him first because she was laying on top of him crying. When the doctor came he said that Jim was covered in vomit and he was very lucky. This time his wife had given him too much poison and it had upset his stomach and caused him to vomit it out. The doctor went on to explain that unfortunately Jim had ingested enough poison that it went through his entire system and caused paralysis in most of his body. The doctor said Jim would never walk again.

Jim was now a single paralyzed father. But, Jim was a survivor and with the love and support of those who loved him he did walk again. He walked and he worked and he provided for his family. One might wonder what he would have thought if he knew what adventures that were in store when he would receive a letter about a young Italian widow.

"One year we planted a lot of garlic. That's when I learned to "braid" garlic. Garlic braiding is almost a lost art today. Very few people know how to do it. Jim's hands were stiff and curled so he had a difficult time braiding, so he taught me. He would sort them out according to size and quality and put them in piles. I would then braid them. By the end of garlic season we did about a thousand strings. My young hands were cut and calloused from the dry garlic. That was his cash crop."

CHAPTER TWELVE

"Jim had a niece in Kinsman, Ohio. She and her family had a big dairy farm. She raised six boys to work the farm but by now her boys had grown up and left home. There was only one boy left at home that summer. Summer was the busy time and they needed more help. My stepfather and Mary McGill talked and the next thing I knew...about my third or fourth summer here I was working on the McGill Dairy Farm. It was like going from the eighteenth century to the twentieth century. They had the biggest and most modern equipment of the time. They had tractors, trucks, all different kinds of cutting machines, baling machines, hay wagons...it was a different world!

Everything seemed to be on the fast track. It hadn't been but three years since I took that horse and buggy ride from Baia to Naples and all of sudden, I'm in the twentieth century! "

July 1958- Kinsman, Ohio

~

Tony woke up and stared up in the dark. He could barely make out the ceiling fan gently blowing. He sighed and rubbed him eyes. It had to be time to get up. He'd been on the dairy farm for several months by now and had become accustomed to the routine. He had learned by his own body clock when it was 5:30. He began to hear some movement in the halls and he tossed off his sheet. He made his way down the creaky back steps and out the screen door. It slammed gently behind him and he walked across the old wooden porch. He saw a couple of shadows out in the field and started making his way to the cow barn. It was milking time and he knew the drill. He grabbed a bucket and got to work. Milking was done in relative silence. Well, the cows made noises but there wasn't much chatter among the farm hands. Daily milking started at about 5:30 a.m. and by 8:00 a.m. everything was done and cleaned up. Tony made his way back up to the farmhouse, his tummy rumbled as he thought about farm fresh eggs, milk and toast.

Just as Tony sat at the table Mary set a plate of eggs in front of him as if she expected him to sit there. The breakfast table was in stark contrast to the milking barn. Everyone was awake now and full of banter and chit chat. There was a lot to discuss as Mary's son, Roy gave instructions and discussed the day's chores and projects. Just then Tony heard the familiar sound of the milk truck revving around the corner of the barn. He didn't even have to wait for it. Someone would have to go unload the empty milk crates and load the full ones. He looked around the room and everyone was eating like they hadn't even heard the big milk truck.

"Better get out there kid," said Roy. He smiled good- naturedly never looking up from his plate.

"Aww man," Tony sighed dropping his fork, "I hate being the youngest!" But he chuckled as he got up; knowing Mary would keep his eggs warm for him. He sort of liked working so hard on that farm.

Tony liked that there was always something to do on the farm. The morning was full; with milking and cleaning stalls. Lunch was always fresh, hot and on the table. After lunch the crew would go back out and work until 5 and then another hot, fresh meal. Evening milking started at 6 and lasted until 8. Then there was equipment check and fixing any machinery that needed tending to. After that it was pretty much dark and the farmhands would head to the basement to shower and change clothes to be ready for milking in the morning.

"One night after Roy and me got cleaned up I was sitting in a chair having a beer while he was brushing his teeth. When he got done he looked at me and asked "Did you brush your teeth?"

I said "No."

He asked "Why not?"

I said "I don't know, I never do."

He said "Tomorrow morning after breakfast I'm taking you to the drugstore and buying your toothbrush and paste and you're going to start brushing your teeth twice a day."

I explained to him that nobody ever showed me or told me about brushing my teeth. We didn't do it at home. So here I was fourteen or fifteen learning about dental hygiene. We got the toothbrush and toothpaste and for a while he kept an eye on me to make sure I did it."

Roy McGill always kept a good eye on Tony. He had grown very fond of him and on several occasions he even stuck up for him when someone would criticize Tony. Tony wasn't used to that but Roy was very important to him.

Tony learned so many new skills that summer. He could plow and cut fields, cut hay, bale hay, drive dump trucks. It was hard work but he really enjoyed it and was eager to learn. The summer ended and Gemma and Jim came to collect Tony from McGill Dairy Farm. Mary gave Jim $150 and two pairs of jeans. Jim gave Tony the jeans and kept the money.

Tony didn't really have any ideas what he wanted to be when he grew up. He had once read a story about a famous Trumbull County trial attorney named Clarence Darrow. It fascinated him and he wondered if he would be a good trial attorney himself. He went to the library that school year and looked up stories about Clarence Darrow.

The school year was long but eventually summer came. Tony returned the following summer and worked the dairy farm. He loved being there and loved working hard but he was growing up fast and had very little parental supervision. One night he and Roy went to a bar. Tony didn't know how many beers he had but it was more than he meant to and the next day he could barely function. Tony's head was pounding as he looked for a place to rest for a minutes in the hayfield. He spotted the hay wagon and crawled under. The hangover really kicked in and he fell asleep, really asleep. He missed the lunch bell and Roy climbed in and drove the hay wagon back to the house leaving Tony passed out in the blistering sun. When Roy finished his lunch he came back and kicked Tony. "Come on, we got work to do" He said walking away. Tony didn't touch beer for a long time after that.

As the summer came to a close and fall was setting in, Roy offered for Tony to stay in Kinsman and go to school but Tony was ready to get back to his life in Hubbard. He was about 16, had lost most of his Italian accent and was able to blend in with the other kids. He looked forward to American high school life in Hubbard.

CHAPTER THIRTEEN

1959- 1961 Hubbard Ohio

~

The walk into Hubbard was about 5 miles and Tony and some of the neighborhood kids would "get creative" about getting to Hubbard and other nearby towns. There were railroad tracks right behind the house and Tony, Jerry, George and Dickey used to jump the train, hitch a ride to Sharon, Pa, catch a movie and hitch a ride back. They would usually sneak into the movie and sneak in food and drinks.

The mischievous foursome was relentless in their antics. On warm summer nights they would hurl rotten tomatoes at the train workers who were sitting on the caboose deck, breaking their glasses and knocking them off their chairs.

"Another time it was a nice warm night and me and Dick were on the side of the road and Jerry and George were on the other side just waiting for someone. That evening was warm like I said, so the person who was driving had their windows down (we didn't have air conditioning back then). As the vehicle came in range we let them have it with rotten tomatoes. The driver slammed the brakes on, got out of the vehicle, with rotten tomatoes hanging off her and the inside of her car and let out one blood curdling scream. "Dickey! Georgie! Get your asses home!" All I heard was Dickey say "Oh shit, that's our mother!" Everybody scattered! Dickey and George ran through the woods and fields to beat their Mom home. I ran home to mine. Dickey and George were grounded for a long time after that stunt.

"Another time me and John Yohman had a kid from Chestnut Ridge Road in the garage and told him we were going to hang him because he was making fun of my sister, Rachel. The kids started crying and promised he wouldn't do it again so we let him go. You should have seen him run. "

Hubbard-Masury Road - 1963

~

Early one morning Tony woke up to the sound of a knock on the door.

"Get up and get dressed, we're going on a trip." The voice of his stepfather sounded very stern.

Tony got up and got dressed and walked out into the hallway. His little sister Rachel was being escorted by his mother down the hall and down the stairs. Tony noticed Rachel had on a new dress and new shoes. She looked at him with her big brown eyes as she passed.

"You look pretty." Tony whispered and she smiled up at him. She was about seven but she was not as advanced as she should be. His twin sisters Delores and Gina appeared and asked where they were all going.

"We're going on a trip," said Jim. "Go get in the car while I get your mother.
"

Tony, Delores and Gina got in the car and watched the front door. Gemma appeared with Rachel and Jim helped them over to the car and got them in. Tony wondered who they were going to visit. It felt like a Sunday visiting day when they would go and see someone they knew for the day, only this was not a Sunday. They rode in silence for about a half an hour and they pulled up in front of a big official looking building. Tony had no idea where there were and started to get nervous. Just then a Sheriff's car pulled up and the Sheriff got out. He talked to Jim in a very hushed, low voice. Tony's heart began to beat in his chest.

'They're sending me to reform school!" he thought and considered running as fast as he could. Before he could make a move the Sheriff took Rachel by the arm and put her in the back of a car.

'Rachel?' Tony thought, 'What had Rachel done?' She was just an innocent little girl. A very innocent little girl! Rachel began to scream and Delores and Gina were crying and screaming. Tony ran up to the driver

"Where are you taking my sister?" he pleaded.

"She's being transported to Columbus; she's State property now kid," he said and looked straight ahead.

Rachel was screaming "Daddy! Daddy! I want to go home!" Tony felt completely helpless. He realized then why she had the new dress and shoes. He glared at his mother and stepfather. How could they!

Nobody would explain anything to Tony, Delores or Gina but Tony figured it out somewhat on his own in reflecting back. When Rachel turned 6 Jim took her to the Chestnut Ridge School. Rachel had no social skills, had a hard time speaking, had very poor muscle coordination and was obviously mentally and physically challenged. Often Jim would be called to the school to come and get her and take her home to clean her up after she'd soiled herself. Tony figured the school principal and his stepfather had made some arrangement for her to be taken away. It was the worst thing Tony could think of doing to a little girl like that.

"That summer we went to visit her in Columbus. It was a state run school with big stone buildings, and stone walls around it. The buildings were damp, dark and cold. It seemed like a free for all atmosphere. It was all different ages, different IQ levels all thrown in together. We would take Rachel out for a few hours, bring her to White Castle Hamburger, eat a few hamburgers and then have to take her back. That was the hard part. Her Dad never said anything but it had to be exceptionally hard on him. All she kept saying was "Daddy Daddy I want to go home!" As I look back I don't believe she realized what she was saying. It was a phrase she carried her whole life "I want to go home."

Usually we would make that trip once a year. That was before the interstate highway system. Back then we would get on Route 62 in Hubbard and take it all the way to Columbus. It was boring, depressing and frustrating. It frustrated me to see how people were treated. Today I believe somebody would go to jail".

Life on Hubbard Masury Road in those days was difficult on the best of days and Tony's life was fraught with situations and events most kids today would never experience, or at least they shouldn't. Tony remembers Jim telling him to get his gun when the neighbor's dog was in their yard. Tony watched in horror as his stepfather matter-of-factly shot the dog and then told Tony to put the gun away and bury the dog by the railroad tracks.

"On another occasion we were in the garden and in the back of a neighbor's house. There was a pear tree which was loaded with fruit. It was also loaded with blackbirds eating the fruit. Again he told me to get the shotgun. I gave him the gun...I'm wondering 'What's he doing?' BAM! I'm asked to put the gun away, get a basket, go to the tree and get the dead birds. We cleaned them, cooked them and that was our dinner that night. "

1964 – Hubbard, Ohio

~

Before Tony knew it he was a senior in high school. By this time he had given up on his dreams of being a lawyer. He pretty much just wanted to "get by". He realized too late that he was not going to graduate from high school as he was one credit shy. He blew it off and figured he would just get a job. He was, as was said, comfortable with the status quo.

Tony once again found himself out in Kinsman, Ohio. This time he had been hired to work at McGill Septic making septic tanks. He earned enough money to buy a used car, give his stepdad some money to help around the house and a little spending money for beer, which he had forgiven for leaving him passed out in the scorching sun in a field.

McGill Septic had a lot of big, often dangerous equipment. They used torches and welding equipment in the process. One day a young man named Sonny from a few houses down the road came and asked to use the burning torches. He had found a double barreled shotgun and told Tony he wanted to modify it to make a handle. It didn't make any sense to Tony but that was what he said he wanted to do. Tony watched as Sonny lit the torches. Just as Tony turned to walk away he heard a loud blast. He turned back to see Sonny get blown off the ground and back. Tony ran back to him and could see him turning white. He crouched down to help Sonny who was holding his stomach. Tony could see his guts were showing through a big hole. He covered Sonny with his coat and ran to call an ambulance. As he got back he could see that Sonny was fading. He tried to keep him warm but Sonny was in really bad shape. Tony could hear the sirens of the ambulance entering McGill Septic just as he watched Sonny die there on the ground. Alive one minute and gone the next.

"That incident pretty much showed me that when your time comes, it comes. What are the odds of finding a loaded shot gun barrel in a gravel pit?

A few days later when I went to the funeral service, it was one of the hardest days of my young life. To walk in and see wife and young kids there was very painful. You could clearly see the pain in his parents' faces. As his father and I were talking he asked me different questions about what happened. I responded the best I could and as I was leaving I thought 'It must be so hard to bury a son, I hope I never have to do that.'
"

CHAPTER FOURTEEN

It was a hot summer afternoon and Tony and Jim were pulling weeds from the garden. The garden was enormous and had rows and rows of everything and anything that would grow in Ohio and feed a family. The weeding was never finished. Once you finished one row it was time to go back and start again.

The sun was beating down on Tony but he was used to it. He stood up to stretch his back and noticed a big car pull into the driveway. Three men got out of a big, black car as Tony watched curiously. Two of the men were dressed in suits and one man was dressed more casually. Tony stared and fears of reform school fleeted through his mind. 'I'm a grown man.' He thought and puffed up his chest. The men walked up the lawn to the garden and Tony heard them begin to call out.

"Aren't you going to say hello to your uncle?" One of the men shouted. Tony's eyebrows raised in disbelief as he recognized his Uncle Modesto.

"Hey there kid," Said Uncle Modesto giving Tony a big hug. It was so great to see him and yet so surreal. Tony had pretty much lost all contact with his family in Italy by this time but it was so nice to see him. They spent the afternoon catching up and telling stories.

Uncle Modesto had brought his whole family from Italy to Canada and he was now living in Toronto with wife and two sons, Antonio and Mario who were born in Italy. He had come to visit some relatives in Elwood City and started asking around if anyone knew of Tony's whereabouts. Someone must have told him because there he was, in the flesh, his Uncle Modesto standing knee deep in tomato plants on Hubbard-Masury Road. Tony couldn't imagine anything nicer. That evening the two exchanged addresses and Modesto promised to keep in touch. They hugged warmly as they parted and Tony hoped Uncle Modesto would keep him promise. He did.

"By February of that year my Stepfather got real sick. He was in and out of the hospital and by March he had passed on. When it came time to take care of all the legal paperwork it was a real mess. There was my mother who could not read or write or speak English, my two younger sisters who were eight years old and me. I could read and write but there was no cooperation between me and my Mom. One day I had to go to the Trumbull County Courthouse to take care of some legal papers about the house. I came to find out that my stepfather had many aliases. I thought he was Jim Condi...well on some papers it was Jim Cunti, some Vigenzo Conti, some James Conti. It was a real mess.

While I was at the Courthouse I thought I had better make sure I had been adopted and had the right name myself. When all was said and done I learned that I had not ever been adopted and my name was wrong on all my documentation; my Army draft card, my drivers' license, my Social Security Number, everything was wrong. It was a nightmare to straighten everything out. Mind you, I had gone all through school as Tony Condi.

In the meantime I was drafted into the Italian Army. No way in hell I was going back to Italy so I had to do some serious paperwork to take care of it fast! As I was working on getting my name situation straightened out I was also applying for U.S. Citizenship before I got deported or sent to the Italian Army. I finally got to take my test to become an American citizen, passed it and I was officially an American citizen, with the correct SS number, correct drivers' license, correct draft card and most of all the correct name Antonio DiTommaso. The American dream at it's best."

Tony's mother and he were at each other's throats by this point. She was a forty two year old, twice widowed immigrant with two little girls and no way to support herself. She couldn't speak any English and she had a very unruly son. That would be hard on the very best of people.

They would argue day and night. Sometimes Gemma would lock Tony out of the house. She did not allow him to have a key and sometimes he would have to go and sleep on his stepsister Minie's couch or a friend's house. On many occasions he even slept in his car. One night she put all Tony's clothes on the front porch and he made plans to go live at the YMCA. Minie wouldn't have it and she set Tony up in Chuck's room with him. Tony was working and was able to give her a few dollars a week for rent and food.

Tony had met a girl from Girard named Dianna that spring and they had been dating quite seriously. Tony decided to take his girlfriend to meet his Aunt Matrona in New Castle. After some small talk Aunt Matrona asked Tony if he planned to marry Dianna. He said they had talked about it. Aunt Matrona asked a few key questions and in very clear English said "Not Italian, no money you're marrying the wrong woman." Tony was quite shocked. He knew his Aunt had a sharp tongue but he thought she was way out of line. They finished dinner, thanked his Aunt and never went back again.

Tony had made a very close friend in high school. His name was Denny Norris and they did everything together. Denny had moved from the South Side of Youngstown to Hubbard in ninth grade. It was the kind of friendship that when you hit it off you just know that you will be friends for life. Denny was a person Tony could confide in and trust and he knew that he could tell him anything.

One day after work he and Denny stopped for a sandwich. They were sitting and talking just as they had always done. He felt so comfortable with Denny. He looked at him as Denny was telling some story or another. Tony looked at him very seriously and Denny stopped.
"What?" he asked cautiously.
"I think Dianna is pregnant," Tony blurted.   Denny's head dropped.
"What are you going to do?" Denny asked.
"I don't know, get married I guess, " Tony said carefully.
"What are you stupid? You're either going to get married or not, it's not something you guess!' He stared at Tony for a while. "Have you thought about an abortion?" He looked at Tony for a reaction.
"No," Tony said instantly.
"Why not?" Denny said warmly

"You wouldn't understand," Tony said. He couldn't get that mental picture of Uncle Pepino beating his mother out of his mind. At the time he didn't realize what that was all about but now, as he was older he realized Pepino was trying to cause Gemma to have a miscarriage. 'No', he thought to himself. ' I won't do that to my baby.'

"Shortly after we started to make some plans, found an apartment and bought some furniture. We went to West Virginia and got married. When we came back I was ready to start a whole new phase of my life. In September I became a father. To be honest I never gave it much thought. Today everybody would be at the hospital; Grandparents, friends, brothers and sisters. Back then Dianna was in the delivery room and I was alone it the father's waiting room, pacing and waiting. Finally a nurse came out and called for the father.
"DiTommaso!' she announced.
"That's me," I said nervously.
"You have a son, would you like to see him?"
"Yes, I would."
"Follow me," she said going back through the double doors.

When I first saw him he wasn't cleaned up yet. What a sight! But in a few days I was able to bring him them both home and I started yet another life. Now I had a son to take care of."

Tony and Dianna named their first born Antonio Jr. in the classic Italian tradition. By January of 1967 the young couple welcomed another son, Joseph John and by July of 1968 they welcomed a third son, Michael. That June they bought their first house . It was small but a good starter home. Tony worked hard earning for the family and Dianna went to classes so that she could become a Catholic and they could be remarried in they eyes of the Catholic church and baptize their boys. They were remarried at St. Bernadette's in Masury.

By this time Tony had been hired on with a good union contractor in Youngstown. There were some rocky times with talk of strikes and Tony had 3 boys to feed and 1 on the way. He did what he could to put food on the table. He worked for that company most of his adult life.

In September of 1974 Dianna gave birth to a fourth son and they named him Daniel. The young couple did their best and by this time had bought a bigger house with some acreage. The marriage however, was strained by many of the things of life that strain a young couple's marriage and by 1980 they admitted that they could go on no longer. Tony sat his boys down and had the hardest conversation of his life. They all cried and Tony tried to explain. Divorce is unexplainable. Tony was heartbroken and that day he moved out.

Tony's life began to spiral out of control that summer. He stopped paying on the credit cards, drank heavily, ignored letters from creditors and went from building his American dream to seemingly trying to destroy himself.

"I don't care how much you try to sugarcoat a divorce. A divorce is a divorce. It's a painful thing for everybody. It's painful emotionally and financially.

One day I came home to my apartment and there was a Trumbull County Sheriff with a letter in his hand outside my door. I knew if I turned around he was coming after me so I kept walking up to my door. I knocked (knowing no one would answer) knocked again, turned around and looked at the Sheriff.

"Are you looking for Tony?" I asked.

"I am looking for Antonio DiTommaso," he said sternly.

"Well you got the right place, I'm looking for him too. He owes me money but I can't seem to catch up to him," I said. "I hope you find him. Have a nice day," I said. I turned around and walked to my car, got in and left. So much was going on in my life and I thought 'What's next?' "

It was late summer of 1980. Tony pulled into the home of his good friends Paul and Joanie. Tony and Paul were sitting in the kitchen talking. He had known Paul for years and was very comfortable with him. The two friends were engaged in conversation when they noticed her standing in the doorway. They both looked up to see Joanie with tears in her eyes. Paul and Tony stood up and moved toward her. She was white as a sheet.

"What is it Joanie?" Paul asked taking her hands.

Joanie shuddered "I've just been on the phone with Dianna. I have some bad news," she looked right at Tony.

"Well, what is it? How much worse can it get?" Tony said bracing for whatever she was going to say.

"Denny's dead," she blurted out.

"What?" Tony's legs felt like rubber.

"Denny got killed last night, I'm so sorry Tony," she cried.

Tony let out a scream and slid down the wall. Paul went to the liquor cabinet and poured a shot. He brought the whiskey over to Tony who drank it immediately. Paul and Joanie left Tony alone in the kitchen on the floor, where he stayed for some time. Paul, worried about Tony eventually came back in.

"Is there anything I can do? Anything," His offer was sincere but futile.

"No," Tony got up and left.

He could hardly see the road through his tears as he drove to his apartment. His best friend...dead. It hardly seemed real at all. Once home, he called Denny's sister who told him Denny hit a tree head on. Tony drank a half a bottle of whiskey. He drank until he fell asleep. It seemed all hope was lost and his American dream was slipping through his fingers.

CHAPTER FIFTEEN

Hubbard, Ohio 2014

~

Tony sat in silence on his pack porch. His mind raced. Could it possibly be that the women he remembered from the ship had been living down the road for sixty years? Sixty years? Nah, it would be impossible. That woman who had helped him got in a different line and went to a different town. Didn't she? Thinking back sixty years is not easy, especially when much of it you have chosen to forget. Jack was arranging a meeting.

What if it was her? What if the woman who had stepped up to be his guardian and accompanied him on that big ship had lived down the road in Lowellville all this time. The idea of seeing her again filled his heart with hope. A connection, a bridge to his past. Someone who remembers to share the memory. Someone to share the story that had burdened his heart all these years. He would wait. He would wait and not play it out in his mind. He would just accept whatever happened. He could not help however, the glimmer of hope in his heart.

He smiled to himself and got up. He ran his hands through his gray hair and went down the basement steps to the cellar. He pulled the lid off the large pail of grape juice or "must" and the familiar smell of fermenting wine hit his nose. He had a vision of Grandfather dancing above him in the wine barrel. "Drink! Now stomp!"

Tony smiled as the memory faded.

CHAPTER SIXTEEN

Hubbard, Ohio 1980's

~

Tony had a really hard road in the early eighties but along with the hard knocks came some really nice things too. He had been frequenting the Bob Evans restaurant on Belmont Avenue and a certain young waitress had caught his eye. They started talking more and more and became quite good friends. Patty was a single mom with a daughter named Missy and the two related on many levels.

One day Tony took his nephew Chuck to Bob Evans for coffee. Patty was just getting off her shift and she came over and sat with the two men for a little while before heading home for the day. Once she had left Chuck smiled at Tony with an inquisitive look.

"Is that your girlfriend?" he asked.

"Her! Hell no, that's the Pope's sister!" Tony exclaimed.

Through their conversations Tony knew that Patty was a Christian. He wasn't really sure how he felt about God or religion. A lot of things had happened to him in his life to make him question the existence of a loving Creator as Patty seemed to see God.

Over the next few months however, the two became more and more fond of each other and Tony worked up the nerve to ask her on a date.
To his surprise she said "Yes."

The two began to see each other on a regular basis despite their obvious differences. Tony's 4 boys got to know Patty's daughter, Missy and the two families eventually became very comfortable with each other.

In January of 1987 Tony and Patty were married. The 3 oldest boys were grown up but Tony and Patty made a home together and brought in Missy and Danny.

Things seemed to really speed up then. Missy graduated from high school and joined the Navy. Danny followed suit after the three older sons and joined the Carpenter's Union. Tony continued to work as a carpenter sometimes alongside his sons throughout the 90's.

By the fall of 1997 Tony got very sick. He didn't know what was wrong but ended up being admitted to the hospital. The doctor's did a lot of tests and said there was something wrong with his liver. It turned out that he had auto immune hepatitis which had cause cirrhosis of the liver. Tony was told that he needed a liver transplant or he could be dead in five years.

Tony waited for the call that they had a liver donor and Patty prayed.

"Patty said "When you're in a hole you can only look up." She prayed for me, she had her friends at church pray for me. I started to go to church. I started going up front for prayer and in about a year's time they took me off the liver transplant list. I was feeling better everyday. I believe it was the good Lord Himself who healed me".

Tony went on to serve on several overseas missions trips. It seemed a crazy thing to do at first but when he thought about all the Lord had seen him through he knew he owed it to the Lord. He also realized that God had not brought him all this way to leave him. So, with equal measures of courage and peace Tony went to Ukraine, Belize and Central America to do carpentry work for the Lord.

In 1999 Tony retired from carpentry and Gemma passed on to the vineyard in the sky. About a year later Tony and Patty decided to take a trip back to Baia. He wanted her to see the town and understand the stories he had told her from her own perspective.

"After forty six years I felt like I had made a complete circle. To see my aunts and uncles, cousins and the town itself was incredible. A lot of the people I recognized. I went to see where my ancestors were buried. Not many people get to experience a feeling like that in their lifetime."

Tony was settling into his retirement and enjoying watching his grandchildren grow completely unaware that the worse experience of his lifetime was about to hit. In November 2002 his youngest son Daniel died. It was something he would never get over. After all that he had seen and experienced in his life this was the deepest hurt, the deepest wound. It was too painful to live and too painful to relive.

"I don't care what you do or what you say, it's always with you."

Tony DiTommaso came to this country a poor 10 year old immigrant with nothing but the clothes on his back. He had little more than his sheer will to live and his determination to build his American life. He raised four sons and a stepdaughter he considers his own. He helped raise his Grandson Todd who has flourished and succeeded.

He watched as his son Tony and wife adopted a Russian baby who is now a man with hopes and dreams of his own. His son Michael married a beautiful Italian Irish girl who lights up a room and they have built a life together. He witnessed the birth of three Grandchildren from his son Joe and wife Elysha. Joey, Kelsey and Josh are all grown up and achieving their own dreams.

In January 2014 Tony achieved the incredible status of Great Grandfather with the birth of his first great grandchild, Kayden. No man has ever loved and adored his family more.

Tony suffered great loss and he achieved great and mighty victories. All through the journey he had always felt in the back of his mind as though he had been alone. He realized in his 71st year that could not have been more wrong.

Looking back on his life Tony realized that he had more guardians that he could count. His mother and his father, his aunts and uncles in Italy, the porter on the train, Jim, Charley, all of his American family, Roy, Mary and Ms. Ryser....but wait, there was one special one he couldn't wait to thank.

June 2014 - Lowellville, Ohio

~

Antonio pulled into the driveway of the home of Gerbina DiRienzo in Lowellville. He clutched fresh flowers in one hand and a bottle of homemade wine in the other. What if it wasn't her? What if it was her? His mind and heart raced with anticipation. What do you bring the woman who made the passage to your new life possible? Since arriving in America he had four sons and step daughter he considered his own. He now had five grandchildren, a great-grandson, 3 daughter in laws and countless friends he loved dearly.

Since arriving in the United States Tony's collective family table had grown to include many other nations. Through the marriages of his sons and births of new members, his immediate family legacy now included, Russia, England, Puerto Rico, Ireland and Cuba. He had indeed achieved his American dream and even made that dream possible for his descendents for generations to come. As he looked up to the house he thought about Gerbina's role in his life. He knew that he was almost turned away from that ship for lack of a guardian. Where would he be without her?

He smiled at Patty and took a big breath, his heart racing. She gave him a reassuring smile and nodded. He stepped out onto the driveway and looked toward the house.

"Hello!" he called up to the woman on the porch who stood with her hands over her mouth. He knew immediately it was her and he felt as though his heart would burst. She recognized him and gasped as tears came to her eyes. She hurried down the stairs and as quickly as her legs would go she hurried over to Tony. The two stood and stared at each other before the giant, inevitable hug and the sound of gleeful laughter filled the street.

Sixty years almost to the day. Sixty years they had lived several miles apart never knowing the other was so close. He had driven by that house a hundred times. Gerbina took Tony and Patty by the hand and hurried them up the stairs to her home. She giggled as she brought them through the kitchen into the dining room where she had laid out many pictures, drinks and food.

The two old friends spent the afternoon introducing their families, looking at old ship records and photos and joyfully sharing the details of their journey. They talked about all that had happened after they parted ways on that dock in Ellis Island that June afternoon in 1954. Gerbina could not take her eyes off Tony. He had changed a lot but she recognized that small boy. That boy that she had longed to see again for so many years. That boy she had dreamt about so many times. She stared at him and her heart was full as he smiled and laughed and told her all about his family and the life he had in America.

Something very special happened to each of their hearts during that reunion. A healing that was sixty years in the making. Somehow it had changed the years that had passed. The healing was retro-active. They had both traveled alone and had no one to share their memories of the dock at Naples or the voyage. They had both experienced the indescribable experience of Ellis Island upon their arrival and stepping on American soil. They had been silent for so long and yet they had never been alone either in the journey nor in the memories.

Antonio and Gerbina had a destined encounter on the dock in Naples all those years ago. The two virtual strangers traveled 4500 miles together and experienced an incredible adventure of epic proportions to the new world; a journey so unique it was almost pointless to discuss it with others who weren't there. Sixty years later, due to an unlikely chance conversation, a silent, unspeakable bond was reaffirmed. As the incredible reunion continued and they both knew they would never be separated again.

Tony DiTommaso realized that without his guardians his journey would have ended at many different times many years ago. Gerbina made the passage across the sea possible but most importantly he realized that he never walked one step without the Lord's grace and covering. It was the Lord who allowed the good things and the bad things. It was the Lord who sent each and every guardian. Every time a guardian stepped out and new guardian stepped in. The truth of that became absolutely, undoubtedly clear as Tony wrote his memoirs. The journey had come full circle, a healing had taken place and for each guardian he will be forever grateful.

"I took me a long time but I finally realized the only way I was able to survive was through the Lord's blessing and guidance. "

DEDICATION FROM TONY DITOMMASO, SR.

I would like to dedicate this story to my children, grandchildren, great grandchildren, and future generations to come.

Personally, I would like to thank my daughter-in-law, Suzie for all the time, hard work and dedication. Suzie, thank you. I love you, Dad

ABOUT THE AUTHOR

Suzanne DiTommaso is married to Tony's oldest son, Tony, Jr. They have a son who is named Vito.

If you would like more information, would like to see family photos or would like to contact the family please follow us on facebook. Guardian - A true story.

Made in the USA
Monee, IL
13 December 2021